Cows

By Cameron Macintosh

What can you tell me about cows?

What do they eat?

How do they sleep?

Let's find out!

“Cow” is the name for a girl cow.

A boy cow is called a bull.
Some bulls have pointy horns
on their heads.

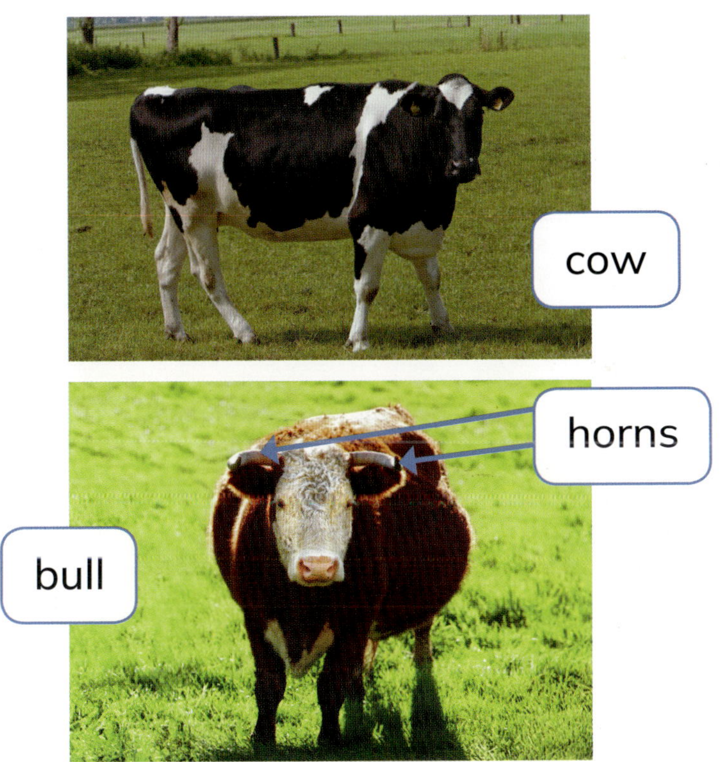

Some cows live on farms.

People ride horses
to round up the cows.

It’s a big job!

Cows have hooves.

A hoof is split,
like two big toes that are joined.

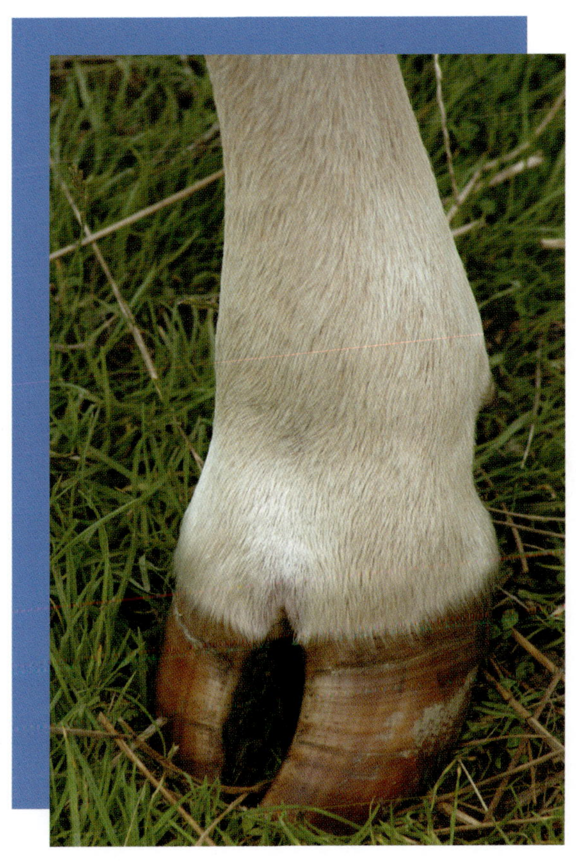

Cows can be white, black or brown.

Their coats can be short or long.

Cows see from the sides of their heads.

Cows bow their snouts down, and then they can see all around.

Cows eat a lot!

They eat things like hay and soybeans.

A cow's tummy has many parts.

Each part helps digest the cow's food.

Cows enjoy joining other cows in a herd.

Cows make noises that sound like “moo”.
That’s how they speak to each other!

Cows get joy from playing around with toys, like balls!

Cows enjoy short naps, too. They lie down on the ground.

Now you have found out so much about cows!

CHECKING FOR MEANING

1. What is a cow's hoof like? *(Literal)*
2. What do bulls sometimes have on their heads? *(Literal)*
3. Why might cows need to eat a lot? *(Inferential)*

EXTENDING VOCABULARY

hooves	What is the singular form of the word *hooves*? What are some other words we use for animal feet?
digest	Read the word *digest*. *Digest* means to break down food into tiny pieces in your stomach. What else might your stomach digest?
noises	Read the word *noises*. What are the sounds in that word? Which letters make the /oi/ sound?

MOVING BEYOND THE TEXT

1. What foods do you eat that come from cows?
2. A female cow is called a cow, and a male cow is called a bull. What other animals have different names for males and females?
3. How is a cow's tummy similar to yours? How is it different?
4. What other animals might you find on a farm? What noises do they make?

TIME TO WRITE

Write about all the things you now know about cows.

PRACTICE WORDS

cows
how
out
about
cow
pointy
round
joined
boy
brown
snouts
around
down
bow
joy
enjoy
toys
cow's
soybeans
noises
joining
now
ground
let's
it's
snout
found
sound
that's